[handwritten inscription: "Best always Robin to Da..."]

M000207021

'Influence'
Over Coffee

How to Gain It or Use It

In Social Media

By Carlos Sapene and Dana C. Arnett

Copyright © 2016 Carlos Sapene and Dana C. Arnett

All rights reserved.

ISBN-13: 978-0692714539 (Wicked Bionic, LLC)

DEDICATION

This book is dedicated to our partners, Suzanne and Edward, our families, friends, employers and clients past and present. Without them we wouldn't be here – really.

Special thanks to Misty McAfee whose editing and organizational skills got us on solid footing, and to Jody Onorato for assisting us.

CONTENTS

FORWARD

After more than thirty years in television and success at the top of my field, I found myself yearning for a new career adventure. Then out of the blue came digital marketing. Well along came Carlos Sapene – who is, among other things, a brilliant, creative, innovative digital marketer. He already had over a decade of experience as an executive in digital at E!, Bravo and the Style Network. With my business experience as an executive in reality television and Carlos's immense digital marketing and IT background, we created Wicked Bionic, a digital agency based in Los Angeles. People ask us why the name "Wicked Bionic". Like every other person looking for a company name that is cool and more importantly has an available domain, I thought the word 'Bionic' was representative of something indestructible. After all, The Six Million Dollar Man and The Bionic Woman were…bionic. Carlos thought 'wicked' was cool and my partner at home is from New England and everything there is 'wicked' something.

Though Carlos and I have backgrounds in entertainment, at Wicked Bionic we work with clients in many industries like technology, healthcare, small business, non-profit, real estate, politics and of course, television. Our main focus is to drive consumers to a product or brand and we do that through social media strategy, target marketing, SEO (Search Engine Marketing), advertising and working with data.

In our first book we wanted to explore the topic of 'influencers' and their impact on marketing and content strategy. Carlos and I (with our Venti cups of caffeine) sat down to assess the use of influence in traditional marketing and it's evolution into the digital space. We wanted to examine the countless ways brands can use influencers to help their product and how making the wrong influencer selection can harm the overall message. We also wanted to define what makes an influencer and understand how and why influencers have influence.

From the people who think they can instantaneously become an influencer to the people who stumbled upon influencing millions by being themselves, we discuss the importance of authenticity in today's culture and how to find your passion.

Grab a cup of coffee, sit down and let's begin the conversation.

- Dana

1
THE EVOLUTION OF INFLUENCE

Dana: In one way or another, someone or something influences all of us, whether it's through traditional marketing or online marketing.

Carlos: We've all been influenced in some way. Even if we lived alone on an island somewhere, we would be influenced by nature. If you think about it, there's always been an influencer for every influence. Throughout history, influence has been at the forefront of, amongst other things, change and creativity. How many people were influenced by Albert Einstein's theories, or by the teachings of Jesus or the innovations of Steve Jobs? Who in turn influenced them?

Dana: Recently I was reading an article by Richard Branson and in it he mentioned, "The biggest, the greatest influencer in my life was my mother." He's such a unique and creative person – I love that he credits his mother. Reading his daily posts on LinkedIn, I see his level of engagement via social media and it's impressive. He's influencing others constantly.

Carlos: Richard Branson's example is great. If we look back at our childhoods, the first influencers in our lives were usually our parents. We looked up to them and they were the people we were modeling our principles and morals against. Then as we began growing into our teens, we began looking at other sources of influence that more closely resemble our understanding of our environment and those who aligned with what we thought and felt. That's when we start to rebel against our initial influencers because we are exposed to other options. It leads to an understanding of how we become influenced. We allow ourselves to be influenced by people when those people, their thoughts, their paths, align with thoughts and feelings within us - with beliefs that we have and that maybe they are able to translate for us. With that, we shift our thinking to be in line with what another persons thought construct may be.

Dana: If I have been influenced by someone who I may perceive as a 'leader', have I now become a 'follower'?

Carlos: The truth is, every influencer is a follower and every follower can be an influencer. People like Gandhi had a huge amount of influence, but even Gandhi was a follower. He followed Hinduism.

Many traditional marketers see influence as measured by reach. The number of followers or audience measures reach but without looking at whether that audience is engaged, attentive and participating; which is what matters most. This concept is derived from the original concept of mass marketing. A great example of this type of marketing is traditional newspapers, where reach is about the level of distribution they had.

Dana: The number of papers sold and the number of distributors informs the success or failure of a newspaper.

Carlos: Yes. Then when you look at television, it's pretty much still based on a ratings system. How many people can be reached? The

Nielsen ratings system from the 1950's was the gold standard for measuring audience size and composition. Many traditional marketers still approach marketing as a measure of 'reach', but the digital space has opened the door to targeted reach, which is completely different. Reach in traditional marketing is defined as the number of potential customers within a large pool that will respond to advertising or a promotional campaign. This is measured by principles like brand recall and brand lift. In progressive digital marketing, 'reach' is the number of people you touch with your marketing message or the number of people that are exposed to your message but it becomes a secondary or tertiary metric. Basically, less important.

Dana: So in the world of influencers, the people who are influencers are not necessarily the people that have the largest reach but are those that are able to speak to a core audience and translate their value exchange to a conversion.

Influencers Need Followers – How Does That Happen?

Carlos: The initial step is to investigate why we follow others. We can't go directly into attempting to be an influencer until we start by understanding how and where we ourselves are followers and who influences us and why. That way you will be able to ask yourself why people would want to follow YOU.

Dana: To begin we look at who has made or makes an impact in our lives. What is it that we like or connect with or enjoy about this person? What is it about them that makes me feel connected? Take some time to watch and evaluate all those that you pay attention to in your day and why. There are so many different levels to who interests us and what about them influences us.

Carlos: People that have real influence, in most cases, possess some kind of passion for something that's of value to them and they share it.

Leveraging Influence

Dana: One of the ways we leverage influence in the digital space is through influencer marketing. It's a business and a big business. One doesn't wake up one morning and decide to be an influencer in the digital marketing space though - it's not a job one applies to and is hired for – it's the process and evolution of developing a voice in a marketplace.

Carlos: There are a lot of people that think, "Oh, I'm going to become an influencer. I'm going to go out there and I'm going to get a huge following." That's the wrong way to go about it.

Dana: It can't be approached as a traditional business with a business plan.

Carlos: A common thought is, "Oh, I'm going to grow a following so I can make money." That's not the way to grow a following. The influence that social media creates is a level of transparency that equals being real. You become an influencer by following your passion, not by trying to 'become' an influencer.

Dana: It's sort of a trust activity to simply follow your passion, express it and if you are being true to yourself, there will be others like you that connect with what you have to say. Will every influencer gather 4 million followers? No, but we have suggestions in this book to discover whether you have something to express in your own voice and the ways to do that. We also hope to help people with businesses, or 'brands' as we refer to them throughout this book, know what to look for and how to use influencers as part of their digital strategy.

Carlos: Becoming an influencer is about doing what you love. That's how so many have become these huge influencers with people following them and without need for large marketing machines behind them. It still surprises people when they see the trajectory of a YouTube star for example.

Dana: I research YouTube often and see what younger people are doing. They're doing so many 'normal' things: being silly, putting on make-up, skateboarding, yelling at each other; they're playing video games, simply talking about anything. I often think, "Why do people find this engaging?"

Carlos: These young people in their teens and 20's are using social media and expressing themselves and it's appealing to their peers. That's not to say that older people aren't also influencers, but there's something really genuine about these young people that really connects them with others. It's the era they were raised in. They're unrestricted. They're fearless. This is what they like. This is what they do. They are going to do it whether anybody follows or not. That's when you open yourself up to being a successful influencer, albeit unintentionally.

Dana: Yesterday I was reading that 29-year-old YouTube star Jenna Marbles' revenue for one year was like 4.3 million. That's 4 MILLION DOLLARS+. At the time of this writing she has over 16.3 million subscribers and many millions of views. She has done this all in less than 6 years. Not to diminish her but sometimes she's simply talking to camera, putting on make-up and other times talking about being hung-over or dating. It's fascinating but from a business standpoint it's really something that she is making that kind of money as an influencer on YouTube. Really?

Carlos: It doesn't make sense to a lot of people because they're not part of her core. Brands aren't always going to understand why someone is so successful at gathering an audience of followers. The great thing about this time in digital is that what these influencers are doing is not traditional advertising. They may not get it but that's not important. What's important is that there are more people who do 'get it' and people relate and listen for their own reasons. Our job is to find out which voice fits the brand and capitalize on that.

Is It Only a Millennial Thing?

Carlos: People keep talking about the Millennial. Millennials (thought to have birth years spanning the early 80's to 2004 or so) are a generation that has grown up in the age of digital and social media. So of course they have led the influencer era and experimented to great success for many. Floating out there is the idea from the older generations that this group is disinterested and presents themselves as smarter than everyone else. Well that's a big generality – it doesn't mean that all Millennials are that way.

Dana: At the opposite end of the spectrum, it's like saying that all retired people are sitting around on their sofas doing nothing. There are retired folks that are on adventures traveling the world and there are those that are sitting on their front porch enjoying the sunset with a cocktail. Generalizations don't work in either age group.

Carlos: Group generalizations take away from the fact that there are individuals in each generation that are having different experiences. If you think about what's important, it's that people identify with something in these influencers, whether that's the majority or the minority.

Dana: It's funny because I was sitting here thinking about the people that are following these young people. Some of these kids are giving a voice to kids that feel goofy growing up or are trying to learn something maybe outside of their small town experience. I sure wish I had someone expressing how awkward I was feeling at that age.

I was at Social Media Week a couple of months back and they had four huge YouTube stars as panelist. One young man mentioned that he went to Las Vegas with his Manager (he had a Manager!) and they pulled up to the hotel where 4,000 13-15 year-old girls were screaming his name. Ice Cube, a celebrity in his '40s, happened to be going into the same hotel, but those screaming girls could have cared less. The YouTube star said it was insanity!

Carlos: Let's talk a little bit about that. I used to work for a large media company. One of the studies we drafted dealt with the reasons why people follow celebrities and why they're so passionate about them. We found that people related to celebrities and considered them friends. They considered them to be people they actually knew.

Our research showed that when you align with a celebrity it's very similar to the way you pick your friends. It's a process of shared beliefs and of being in agreement on certain things. It's the same thing with influence. If you look at it from that perspective, these followers believe that their social media influencers were absolutely aligned with them and they felt like they knew each other.

Can They Be Called Friends?

Carlos: To them, celebrities *are* their friends. They literally would sit there in the studies we did and say, "Oh no. Kim Kardashian would never do that! I know her."

Dana: Kim would never do that.

Carlos: "Yeh, Kim would never do that. I know her and she would never do that." We would say, "When did you actually meet Kim Kardashian?"

They were like, "Oh well, no. I haven't met her, but I KNOW her."

Dana: It really is true. When I was a teenager I knew my General Hospital stars like my closest friends. I *knew* how Luke and Laura would react in any situation.

Carlos: It's crazy but it's normal.

Dana: As crazy as it is, it makes sense, they're in our living rooms or on our devices – in our personal space – day in and day out and we feel we're having interactions with our friends.

Carlos: There's a level of personalization and attachment that happens. People build a persona in their heads that represents the celebrity or influencer based on a mix of perception, individual values and creativity that's expressed. There has been a process, flow and growth to how the Internet has affected mankind and it's reflected in the reasons why influencers have risen on social media and on media overall.

The process, if you think about it, started with the Internet appearing, the early adopters joining it and building the infrastructure that then led to its deployment worldwide. I still remember Katie Couric asking what the Internet was. To think about it today is just incredible. They didn't know what an email was yet. They thought the Internet was an @ back in the day, that you had to go to an '@' something but they didn't even know what '@' stood for.

When the Internet first appeared, it's effect separated humanity instead of uniting it. It was a network that was supposed to join people together with intelligence and learning. It started with universities and research facilities. At CERN the focus was access to information. For the masses though, what it really did in the beginning was create a path and a portal for people to go search out their deepest, darkest thoughts.

Alone With A Computer

Carlos: Because you were alone in a room with a computer, you had a chance to go and explore your deepest, darkest thoughts. Chat rooms became huge because people could discuss what they actually thought with like-minded people and with a layer of invisibility.

Dana: Nobody knew who you were so you could express yourself without fear of being ostracized for being different.

Carlos: Exactly! Porn became huge because people could go on the web and look at porn now without having to go to a video store. Any type of porn. I've always found it interesting that porn is almost always tied to digital innovation.

Dana: No need to hide a dirty magazine under your bed.

Carlos: No more magazines or going into a dark room in the back of a video store. Initially the Internet started by separating humanity. Yet over time, with the rise of social media, it started drawing humanity back together. The medium didn't change, but our consciousness surrounding it changed drastically.

Platforms Designed to Bring People Back Together

Dana: Wasn't Friendster in 2002 the first social platform?

Carlos: Even before Friendster there was Six Degrees in the mid to late '90s, but there were also these chat rooms even before social media. Some of the applications are still around, one of the more popular ones at the time was AIM, AOL Instant Messenger, remember? When AOL was AOL, and CompuServe was still around, like really back in the day. How many people do you think that are reading this book won't even know what these are? It's like a dinosaur of the Internet age now but it is part of the story.

A different communication started surfacing through the use of the Internet. There was that level of connection that started to happen again, and then that connection evolved to a presence like Friendster. Friendster then, sadly, underestimated how fast it was going to grow. It grew so fast that the servers at the time couldn't manage the amount of requests coming in from people trying to get onto the site. A lot of the success and failures, even today, of tech startups has to do with having the right infrastructure at the right time. With the appearance of social media we started to draw people back together, and it started creating these dynamic communities. People that thought the same way, that had the same feelings towards specific factions and were able to join together. It didn't matter that they were all the way across the country.

Dana: Or around the world.

Carlos: From that it then evolved into unique voices standing up in the crowd. There were people that were able to channel the general feeling of a group into something, and then they developed into what we call now call 'influencers'. They were still part of the group, influencers were still part of that general feeling that people had, that attachment that people built to the groups they joined, their voices just began to stand out. Even though the computer kept the distance, the commonality of their thoughts, perceptions and feelings brought them together. There was still a reason why people chose to listen to those influential voices as leaders. It wasn't only them having the loudest voice in the room, it was about them being the most genuine and aligned with honest feelings, perceptions and the thoughts of the group.

Word-of-Mouth vs. Brand Advertising

Carlos: First of all, you trust people you know more than you trust advertising. The reason we've devolved into not trusting advertising is because we've evolved past it. Let's talk about brand advertising first. When search engines first launched they would read the code behind the web pages. You had certain elements that you would place into the code and that would tell the search engine what your site was about. You always needed three basic items; title, description of your site and the keywords. Let's take keywords. If you were a t-shirt site you would enter, 't-shirts, t-shirts for men, t-shirts for women'.

Dana: Three items describing what someone would be looking for in order to find you. Anything that you thought would identify your site.

Carlos: That worked for a while but then, as in most things, some people figured out a way to circumvent and deceive the system and abuse what was intended – we call them the 'black hat' marketers. What happens is that where there are the 'white hat' marketers, there are the 'black hat' marketers.

The white hats are the ones that do things the way they were intended and draw within the lines. The black hats do things that corrupt or abuse the system. So black hats started stuffing the keywords with completely unrelated keywords just so their brands would pop up higher in the ranks for any search, again, trying to focus on reach. They would use words like sex, naked or whatever they thought might be the highest search terms. The idea was, while you're searching for naked people you would stumble upon their t-shirts and buy one.

Dana: The t-shirt brand would pop up higher in the search because they tagged an unrelated keyword that the black hats knew was popular.

Carlos: Right and because they were hoping to trick the search engines. By gaming the system, brands went from aligning with the truth about a brand or creating a perception about a brand to creating a fake perception about a brand, to lying straight up about a brand. This wasn't everybody. Like I said, there are white hats and black hats...

Dana: But there is always somebody that enters and ruins it by trying to abuse the system.

Carlos: There will always be the black hats. Over time, when consumers caught on they began to get suspicious - that's death to a brand. We lost trust in the brands that were attached to those manipulated sites. This happens in every size brand. JC Penney had problems with Google a long time ago because they were allegedly implementing black hat tactics to rank first. When Google found out, you couldn't find JC Penney in something like the first 50 pages of a search engine – that was their punishment.

Dana: Yes, I remember, and Google basically disconnected those search results from them.

Carlos: It all comes back to developing trust in the people and brands that we can relate to honestly and that we don't feel manipulated by. They are the 'people' we think of as our friends and we see our values reflected in them. We see our shortcomings reflected in them also.

Trusting Word-of-Mouth

Carlos: If we're saying that people develop trust and friendship with influencers, then it would make sense to say they develop the same trust by word of mouth from a real friend of theirs. Not only is word of mouth important but also it is usually pretty honest - if there's no agenda. The great thing about word of mouth is that human beings tend to repeat what they hear and if they hear it from someone with authority, they too will replicate it with authority.

Dana: If a friend of mine says that something's good, even before I try it, I'm probably going to say, "You know what, I heard that's really good." A great example is Amazon's Echo. You raved about it and I thought, "I have to get that!" Now I have one at home that I love. A few days later, over a business meeting we begin discussing the benefits of the Echo with our clients at BKF Properties.

Carlos: And what did our clients say?

Dana: Pat said she was now going to get one for everyone on her Christmas list. She had purchased three by the next meeting.

Before we walked in that next day and she had absolutely no idea what it did or how it worked, but we said it was cool. Word of mouth made her do it!

Carlos: After she got them, I believe she said, "I didn't buy it for myself because I don't understand it, but you guys were so excited about it, I just knew my son, nephew and cousin would love it and teach me how to use it."

Dana: That was word of mouth at it's best – to see someone excited about something new and innovative. With all the advertising power behind Amazon, Pat hadn't heard of Echo until we talked about it.

Carlos: We probably just sold Amazon 15 of them. I'm buying their stock today.

Carlos Sapene and Dana C. Arnett

2
BECOMING AN INFLUENCER

Carlos: There is a creative path to becoming an influencer. It starts by identifying what you're passionate about. What do you care about? A lot of people think, "I'm going to go be an influencer in whatever I do for a living since that's what I'm paid to do and what I'm qualified to talk about", something like, "I'm just going to go be one of the best accountants of influence and people will listen to what I say."

Dana: The best accountant…that's funny. You know there's an accountant podcaster?

Carlos: You also can't begin by looking at what other people are doing and where the gap is, the white space you're going to fill. All of those traditional old-time marketing thought processes no longer apply in digital. This new world has a steep learning curve. Traditional marketing was incredibly effective in it's day. Like we've said, it was used until it was abused and a new marketing model had to emerge. Remember the broadcasters of the 50's and 60's that would ask families to gather around the TV?

Dana: Yes, people like Walter Cronkite. He was very trustworthy and I remember my parents took his word as gospel. He was reporting on the state of America.

Carlos: Trustworthy. Magical word, trust. People trusted what newscasters like Walter Cronkite would say and they believed that what they were hearing was the voice of the Nation. Today many news organizations, desperately trying to stay relevant have developed into these unbelievable broadcasts that sometimes are screaming for credibility when they have rushed to air without the time for proper research. There's doesn't seem to be as much time put in for researching anymore. With cable scrambling for ratings, issues often get exploited. So many are jumping the gun to be first; they are not doing the level of reporting that was done back in the day when only a few were reporting.

There are millions of cases in the media now where people have lost their trust and confidence in the traditional delivery of the news. The base of any influence is trust. Trust is something that you build with your followers, you can't force it for ratings and it takes time to develop.

Dana: It's really come full circle – going back to finding those genuine and unique voices that we trust - those influencers that say what we believe. As an influencer, it's about being who you are and trying to send followers the messages that you're passionate about. People are smart; they can tell when you're not being honest.

Carlos: If people hear what you're saying, read what you're saying, see what you're doing on video, on YouTube or wherever, and you're not 'you', you're not being authentic, the dishonesty comes through.

Dana: I think as humans we have an innate ability to smell a rat! Let me act as a person who wants to become an influencer: I've got this idea that I want to share with an audience and I'm not going to be concerned about who's going to pay attention to me, how do I determine which outlet I should use to start sharing content?

Carlos: You don't get to start there, Dana! You don't get to skip to the outlet part yet. Where are we supposed to start?

Dana: Oh yeah, passion...

Ways to Identify Passion

Carlos: The good news and the bad news for the reader is that we can't tell you what *your* passion is but we can help you find it. Either you already know, or if you don't we suggest you start by writing a list of 10 things you feel passionate about. This is the most important part because what you choose matters.

Dana: You're not looking to find the thing that you think no one else is doing yet. And conversely, you're not looking for something because you see other people making money with their experience. It has to be YOUR passion.

Carlos: You're looking at it because it's truly important to you. A lot of people think that they *have to be* an influencer in their particular field because that's what they know best. I used to work in entertainment, which means I should be an influencer for entertainment, right? I'm an expert, right?

Dana: Right. Then I should be an influencer in reality TV post-production.

Carlos: But that's not what it is. What you do for work is not necessarily what you're passionate about.

Dana: You're lucky if it IS your passion!

Carlos: Just because it's what you do for work doesn't necessarily mean it's where your passion lies. That's why it takes some thought and some investigating to find out who you are in your life and what interests you most. It's also important to remember not to be intimidated by others who are succeeding in your passion area. Too many people say, "I'm passionate about dogs, but there are already so many influencers related to dogs."

Dana: "I'll never make a dent. Forget it. It's already being done." That's what I would think.

Carlos: 'It is already being done' is the greatest detriment to innovation. The truth is, the only people you help by not going out there saying and doing what you're passionate about are the people that are already doing it. It's your passion and it doesn't matter that it's also someone else's passion. You have a unique point of view, share it.

Dana: I'm putting money in other pockets is kind of what you're saying?

Carlos: Exactly.

Dana: Because I'm not giving them any competition. It's important to realize it's a big world and there's room for everyone.

Carlos: We're all different. We all have a different voice. The people that follow these influencers are following them for a reason. The people that are going to follow you are going to follow you for a different reason. Also, know that if you want to be an influencer, you're going to be tied to this passion for a long time. You're going to build a core audience around this passion because this is what's supporting your influencer strategy. In other words, you need to make sure that whatever you're passionate about, you're actually passionate about. This concept that comes from traditional marketing of looking for the white space*.

> *****White Space *or* Whitespace** *is referred to as negative space. It's the portion of a page left unmarked, the portion that is left blank, or the empty space in a page. In web design terms, it's the space between graphics, columns, images, text, margins and other elements. Finding the area that no one else is using.*

Carlos: Here's an example of why I feel it's not important to find out if there's a place for you (a 'white space') in social media as an influencer. When I worked in television I remember that in marketing meetings there was always the question, 'what's the white space?'. What are all the other networks not doing? Where should we fit? Where does this show fit in the white space spectrum of other shows? It is the most ridiculous thing to make it your sole focus. Searching desperately for what is NOT being done already.

Dana: What has never been done to this point? Not the best, most innovative show or idea, it's a backwards approach but a long time network method.

Carlos: Listen, I'm not trying to stifle innovation or how one goes about it. But there's clearly a difference between innovating and plugging in white space with any idea you have lying around that may fit it. That sounds like greed more than passion!

Dana: Okay so let's start by giving an example of how to flush out one's passion. Let's use something I love.

Carlos: Right – let's determine what you're passionate about.

Dana: Let's use my passion for dogs.

Carlos: Okay - let's do this exercise with dogs. Here's what you do once you define dogs as your passion. Write down ten things that are related to dogs that you're passionate about.

Dana: All right, my ten items are:

1. Playing with puppies
2. Health
3. Yorkies
4. Personalities
5. Companions
6. Dog Parks
7. Domesticated dogs
8. Dog walking
9. Joy to humans
10. Dog Shows

Carlos: You've listed ten passion points about dogs. Now what I want you to do is stop there and give it a couple of days. Just give it a couple of days and sit with the list. Don't look at it again. In three days grab a sheet of paper and make a new list.

Dana: The same exercise? Ten things?

Carlos: Ten things that you're passionate about regarding dogs. Don't do it based on memory of your previous list. Do it by what you feel in the moment.

Dana: And don't look at the last list?

Carlos: Right. Here's what's important about this exercise: the mood you were in three days ago is not the mood you're in today. Your experiences three days ago are not your experiences today. So we need to compare. Take a look at the two lists to see what items made it on to both lists. Everything that didn't make it on both, you chop off the list. Usually that will leave four or five top core values.

Make Two Lists, Wait 3 Days

Carlos: When you become an influencer in a specific category, you're not an influencer for a day. You're an influencer for a long period of time. You have to identify what your core values are related to and in what you're going to be influential. These core values will sustain you. We are not static beings – every day is new and every day we have different ideas and feelings. There are core values around our passions, which are steady and solid, from that core we can then add additional things that are interesting to us around your passion for dogs.

25

Dana: That's why I wait three days, so I can find out which core values mean the most to me - then I am fluid with the rest.

Carlos: What's going to happen during that time is, you're going to have different experiences. You're going to be in different moods. You're going to be angry one day, happy the next day...

Dana: Annoyed.

Carlos: ...annoyed, thrilled. There's going to be positive and negative emotions with you on those days because that's normal. All of those will influence your passion. Maybe you love dogs but today their barking is annoying you – that's something normal and something to talk about. Your core values will stay consistent through these moods but your day-to-day experiences around those values are what's interesting to share and keeps you and others interested. This allows you the freedom to be authentic.

Dana: From our core grows all the interesting add-ons to that passion. But I see the importance of staying consistent with your core because it's why people first identified with you.

Carlos: Consistency in social media is necessary because, though you may think you are the one choosing to be an influencer, it is in fact your audience that makes you an influencer. They pick you. You don't pick them. When they pick you, they develop a persona for you based on what you are sharing with them. They don't know you, but like we mentioned, they build up this feeling that they know you and that you are their friend.

Dana: I am sharing with others and they are identifying and listening to me. I discover my core values around my passion for loving dogs – then build on that with my day-to-day experiences.

Carlos: Exactly. Make sure you have that persistent messaging because even though your audience picks you to be the influencer, it is up to you what their perception of you will be and the continuity in that messaging is important. Throughout multiple moods because that's how human beings truly live in the world.

Dana: And it's a daily... social media is a daily experience. It's not about sharing once a week about what's been going on. That's no way to draw and keep an audience no matter HOW interesting your passion may be.

Carlos: It's not about once a week, it's about communicating and engaging consistently about what you love. When your audience finds you, begins to trust you, and follows you, you have become an influencer.

3

AFTER THE PASSION

Attraction Not Promotion

Carlos: The social media channel you choose to begin in is going to be based on who your audience is and if they share your similar interests. There are questions that need to be asked to determine that. It would be backwards to pick a social media channel and start sharing there to find your audience.

Dana: If the first step in becoming an influencer is determining your passion, the second step is determining who your core audience will be.

Carlos: What is a core audience? They're the ones who are going to choose to follow you based upon what you have to say. Remember, you don't choose your followers, your followers choose you and you need to find out who they are then determine where they are hanging out. Before we even begin to think of where to express ourselves, we need to ask two questions:

"Who are the people that are going to listen to me?"

"Who are the people that are like me and going to understand what I'm saying and care about it?"

Dana: I think a great example is our client, Adela. She has a unique experience coming from the business she's in and jumping into social media via Periscope*.

Periscope *is a video-streaming app that allows users to view people and their experiences live from around the world.*

Carlos: In Adela's case, which is one of the most non-traditional cases of marketing in the digital age, she was already an established psychic in Los Angeles with a strong clientele. Adela reads people in person and over the phone. However, people on the phone believed she was looking them up on the Internet during the readings. How else would she know these things about them? Some of them thought they couldn't trust her because she claimed to be psychic – they were wary of getting scammed.

A Psychic Challenge

Carlos: The challenge was how to have Adela do what she does but over the Internet while using social media. It's understandable in today's digital age, that unless a psychic is physically sitting across from you, you would suspect them of Googling all of your information.

In order to show that Adela was the 'Real Deal', we started her on Periscope where she created a format for reading people twice a day. On Periscope you're broadcasting live from the app and can't see the other person. You usually don't even know their name, just their handle. The other person sees you, so they can see your hands, they can see your face, and they can see what YOU'RE doing but not the other way around. Adela doesn't get to see their real names, she doesn't get to see their faces or hear their voice (or any stresses in their voice that could give away any information).

She only gets to read their comments or responses as she's doing what she does.

Dana: An unknown audience that she reads blindly.

Carlos: Every time she does a Periscope live reading, there are hundreds of people jumping on her Scope. The platform is very new, but she's been able to parlay it into more business, booking people for full readings. It's become a revenue stream though she did not start out thinking of it as a way to make money. She started by expressing her passion on a fun new app – just talking to people – and an audience found her. She is genuine and likeable and that came across.

Dana: She's been able to monetize her talent using a new tool without trying to go out and make money. It goes back to what we've been discussing, find your passion, be true to who you are and your audience will find you.

Carlos: Adela used Periscope as a tool to do what she loves and what she's meant to do. For years Adela said there were a lot of people of faith who believe that the idea of psychics is wrong. Many people have an apprehension about talking to a psychic simply because they don't understand and there's people that ARE frauds. Periscope enabled Adela to show what she does and what she doesn't do. She's not talking with demons and has no 'tricks' up her sleeve. Adela's been able to reach a core audience of people who appreciate her particular skill.

Dana: People are fascinated with her talent. We see how many people come on Periscope and deluge her with hearts (Periscope's currency). It's the voyeuristic thing you were alluding to earlier about the Internet; people can be a little bit voyeuristic on Periscope without admitting anything about themselves.

One of things I love about social media is that you don't have to have the perfect camera set up. Adela, and others all over YouTube, are not concerned with the lighting or framing themselves perfectly and with a great background. Sometimes there's so much headroom on those close-ups it's hard for me to watch. In my years in television where everything that aired had to be absolutely perfect before going to the network, the majority of social media today would have been un-airable in my television days. The awesome thing now is that no-one cares about all that technical stuff because there aren't really any rules governing how something looks in social media.

Carlos: Another great thing about Adela is that she has an engaging personality. When she's not doing readings on Periscope she talks about being a Mom and funny anecdotes about her kid. Unfortunately, the Internet and people who are not seen aren't always so polite.

Dana: Yes, a challenge came up regarding trolls, but I think we all managed it beautifully. I just love the 'boob story' and specifically how you coached her through it. I think it's indicative of an authentic person reacting in a smart, creative way to 'less polite' folks.

Carlos: Adela is a physically blessed woman and needless to say, several anonymous Periscopers felt the need to repeatedly request visual confirmation of her…'blessings'. Thankfully, Periscope allows you to very quickly block people when you're broadcasting. Initially, Adela blocked people who popped up and asked to see her boobs. I talked to her and I said, 'a lot of them are trolls but a lot of it is also entertainment, and it's part of what you do with them that's going to continue to attract your audience and engage your audience'. Blocking people over and over is distracting everyone engaged in the live feed.

Through her own personality she was able to come up with a crazy solution. As I mentioned Adela is a Mom and therefore has a home filled with toys. One day while Periscoping and being asked to show her boobs she noticed her kids' robot, was sitting close by. Immediately she named him Bob. From then on, every time someone commented and wrote 'boob' she would show 'Bob'.

Meet 'Bob'

Carlos: The people fell in love with Bob! She was ridiculing the stupidity of people trying to deride or distract her on this platform. She managed it so well that we're now selling t-shirts for "Show us your Bob".

Dana: If she goes to the beach and Scopes, she brings Bob and if she Periscopes from the park, Bob is by her side.

Carlos: She takes Bob everywhere! Now she's added other characters to the mix. It's turned into a Mrs. Doubtfire type of show. She brings all these characters that are also a part of who she is and she's turned them into a whole set.

Dana: The best part is, it happened organically.

Carlos: It's real.

Dana: She exemplifies everything we've been discussing, finding your passion and being yourself. If I set out to become a Periscope Star, I would more than likely fail. Adela rolled with it and created an authentic energy. She gained over 2,000 followers organically in her first 2 months.

4
BRANDS AND PERCEPTION

Websites as a Marketing Tool?

Carlos: Websites are a great resource to support your marketing initiatives. People have been conditioned to search the web for information on brands and you want to put forth your best efforts to present your brand in the best way possible.

Dana: But just having a website does not automatically grow a business.

Carlos: It's important to have a website so people who are already aware of you have a place they can visit to learn more. The challenge is a lot of people spend excessive amounts of money and time on making a beautiful website. Or they spend $100 on a website and get something that isn't functional. In either version, there has to be things like SEO (Search Engine Optimization) built into the background to be successful – but that's another conversation! We tell our clients, 'you're not selling a website, you're selling your product or service' and you do that by focusing on the audience. It's definitely a part of what you need to do to have a brand, but it doesn't mean it's the only thing you need to invest in.

Dana: In the old days, you would take out an ad in the newspaper or run an ad in a magazine. You then crossed your fingers and hoped for a return on that marketing investment.

Carlos: It's easy for people to fall into that trap because we keep going back to thinking of marketing in the digital age by overlaying traditional marketing. Again, traditional marketing was about reach and ratings.

Dana: Numbers.

Carlos: The number of readers for the newspapers and magazines, number of homes where they were they were delivered. There're still some out there like the Yellow Pages.

Dana: Why are we still getting stacks of Yellow Pages at my complex? How long does it take until they go into the trash bin?

Carlos: Five seconds...

Dana: I do feel guilty about putting all that paper in the trash.

Carlos: I feel like I'm throwing an entire tree in the trash. Who reads them? Well, I guess there are some people reading them, probably later on in years.

Dana: I live in an older community...a 'later on' community. I think I'm safe in assuming not everyone that lives there is savvy with technology and therefore may need Yellow Pages from time to time... Back to the website – say I've built a beautiful (and affordable) website, where should I spend those marketing dollars to bring people to my brand?

Carlos: A percentage of your marketing budget should be allocated towards working with people of influence in what your brand represents. Let's discuss a bit about brand marketing and how some areas began and have evolved.

The easiest way for a brand to get their message out there, even in traditional marketing, was by word of mouth. People trust other people more than they trust what the brand is saying to them as some brands have used marketing strategies which may be deceiving.

Dana: People are wary of being deceived with brands – we want to be smarter than that.

Carlos: The audience doesn't trust every brand. That's one of the reasons that brands progressed into attaching themselves to celebrities – they capitalized on the reputation of that celebrity and used them to endorse their brand.

Dana: An expensive word-of-mouth strategy for sure.

Carlos: In the beginning it was very smart because many of the celebrities were aspirational – like sports stars. People wanted to be like them and saw them as their friends. People were willing to do whatever 'their' celebrity was doing and buy whatever 'their' celebrity was buying. Nike had huge endorsements. Heck, they still have huge celebrity endorsements. What's happening now though, is that people are looking past that because the audience has become more aware. People understand that something is being sold to them and that the celebrity is endorsing the brand in exchange for money, not because they necessarily believe in the product.

Dana: We realize 'such-n-such' celebrity was paid $5 million to sell me *that* tennis racquet. I sure hope the product is good but now I am skeptical. Don't you know it though, when I go into a store to buy a tennis racquet, I'm conditioned to gravitate towards the racquet with the celebrity endorsement? Somewhere deep down I suspect the others aren't quite as good. That's crazy! I know I'm being manipulated and what do I do? I buy the damn celebrity endorsed racquet!

Carlos: Excellent consumer marketing strategy.

Dana: Having the business mind that I do, I have to congratulate their business team for acquiring a deal that's bringing in a gazillion dollars.

Carlos: Spending marketing dollars on celebrities is still very viable if you're a big league player but it has also become viable to invest those marketing dollars on an influencer. Big celebrities have big price tags but there are many different levels of influencers and less dollars can be spent to drive an audience to your website and product or brand.

Audience and Brand Relations

Carlos: One of the things that changed the marketing landscape was when Reality TV hit the masses. Reality TV today is often everything BUT real.

Dana: Agreed. Reality TV gave me a great career for decades but I have a hard time with how it changed from being unique and genuine to pretty much scripted. In the beginning what reality

TV did really well, was to give a glimpse into the lives of real people and observed them in their world.

Carlos: They showed real people in real life situations and people were captivated. Like everything else, over time producers ran out of interesting ideas. There are now 700 different versions of The Housewives franchise.

Dana: You're exaggerating, there's only like 698 variations.

Carlos: Housewives of Atlanta, Orange County, Beverly Hills, New York, Basketball Wives and so on. They capitalized on a theme and burnt it out. When ideas run out, ideas are recycled.

Dana: Then it evolved into, what the Networks actually did call "scripted reality." Scripted Reality means I'm the producer and I'm going to say how the scene is going to go. I'll push it along to create the story arc we pitched to the network. Previously, talented producers would trust the format and casting. If the scene became boring, the producer would drop a red herring into a scene and observe how people reacted. My boss on "The Biggest Loser" was amazing at that. It was a blast to watch human behavior. It's much different now.

Carlos: Now it's about building situations that the producer decides will be interesting for people instead of letting it play out organically. People are starting to see through the smoke and mirrors.

Dana: Then there are the people who become celebrities out of reality TV.

Carlos: From the digital side, I worked on supporting "Keeping up with the Kardashians". When they first came on the air and for many years after, the show became a huge hit. Initially everyone started watching because they were a genuinely entertaining family with real problems. Real situations happened to this family that were relatable. The show was so successful and people were so interested that they evolved into a brand.

Dana: Now they have the brand to live up to.

Carlos: And as these things always seem to do, there's now distrust from the audience. It doesn't mean people have stopped watching, just the opposite, it's just that most people aren't naïve when they watch. They are knowingly joining the ride.

Dana: It all goes back to trust and to build trust with your audience, be it a celebrity or digital media influencer, you need to be expressing your passion and talking about what you genuinely love.

Carlos: If you're doing what you love, you're going to be honest about how you feel and what you do. You align based on an influencer reflecting the values and message that you desire for your brand. How do you want your brand to be perceived in the world?

The funny thing is that brands at the beginning of, or I guess midway through, social media, were lucky enough that they didn't have to work very hard to get people's attention because people proactively went on brand websites and said, "I like this." I remember some of the bigger brands just having floods of people coming in that liked them. Brands like McDonalds and Coke all of the sudden had a massive captive audience. This is before

Facebook and Twitter fine-tuned their algorithms. When everything you posted about showed up in the feed. Unfortunately, they didn't know what to do with the customer once they logged on or 'Liked' their page. They didn't know how to speak with their clientele because a brand had never talked directly to a customer.

Brands were so used to speaking through a large PR agency that when they received a huge influx of people to their website, they didn't know what to do with them. Not only did they not know how to engage, they were unsure if they should. Once their legal departments got involved and said, "Don't answer", it was over before it began. They lost one of the biggest opportunities on social media which is capitalizing on your audience.

Dana: It was an important industry lesson. Now we understand more about the nature and importance of engagement in the digital space.

Carlos: Some brands realized what they didn't know and were smart enough to hire representation for their brand on social media. They hired social media marketers to answer people and engage them. Some of them hired internal evangelists that knew and loved the brand but maybe were working another role within the company. In turn, those brands saw huge benefits from this approach.

Dana: One of my favorite sayings is 'hire what you don't know'. You can't learn about everything and there are people that know how to do the things that you may not. Hiring agencies that know how to effectively use influencers and market in digital is way more cost effective then trying to figure out how to do something out of your wheelhouse.

Audience #'s Do Not = Automatic Success

Carlos: Aligning your brand with appropriate influencers who can reflect your brand message should also be what makes them the right influencers for their followers. Using the proper influencers to speak in their unique voice about your brand is VERY effective.

Dana: Like the number of followers an influencer has does not guarantee they're the right influencer for your brand.

Carlos: The number of followers that an influencer has does not equal the right audience/influencer for a brand. There's a lot of data out there. There are many ways to collect data and information that enables us to understand the bigger picture around an influencer and their audience. A big part of what we do is assess what's going on around the influencer. We want to understand their audience, what the influencer stands for, what's the reasoning behind their influence, what are their core values. What they're honest about and whether they're perceived as trustworthy. After that process we set about aligning the brand with the right influencer for them and their message.

Nowadays, it's not uncommon to find brands that are going out there and grabbing whoever they can find to talk about their brand. Sometimes they get lucky and end up aligning with the 'right' influencer, but with the number of influencers now, there is a much more tactical approach. This is where being effective at matching influencer to brand is important. In our case, we do the research for the right relationship, which protects budget dollars and the brands image. Money well spent on research beforehand can save millions.

Dana: I read about an anti-smoking campaign that hired influencers from Twitter. Come to find out, several of the influencers were smokers. It was most likely an honest mistake, but it was so counter to the message. Not a good match.

Carlos: And you know who finds out? The people.

Dana: The followers.

Carlos: They're always on the lookout for something disingenuous.

Dana: Not only will the followers find out, but it also doesn't take long. We take particular care when hiring our influencers. We're very clear about each platform and the audience each feeds. There's no issue for us if an influencer is a smoker as long as that doesn't interfere with the message our clients or brand wants out there.

5
ALL FOLLOWERS ARE NOT EQUAL

Carlos: There are three main types of followers:

1. Active   2. Passive   3. Inactive

Active Followers are the ones that are continually engaging. They are always talking, they're replying, they're looking for an answer, they're engaging with your content. They'll be proactive about saying what they're utilizing or whatever it is that you're telling them to do.

The **Passive Follower** is the one that's voyeuristic in nature. It doesn't mean they're inactive though; their activity is just not always visible.

Dana: The ones that only click 'Like,' but don't join the conversation.

Carlos: They may click 'Like,' or they may just read or watch and not respond. They look to see what other people are telling you. They may 'like' the comments of what other people are telling you in your comment section. They don't engage because that's not their personality.

Then there's the **Inactive Follower**, which is a huge chunk of the followers out there. These are the people who checked you out once and heard one thing they liked. They like you, but they never listen.

Dana: They never look at you again.

Carlos: They are purely a one-visit number.

Dana: I'm sure people see a large number of followers and think, "I have half a million followers who like me."

Carlos: Think about it this way, about 20% of the influencers on the Internet drive 80% of the content on social media.

Dana: I like that stat, let's break it down.

Carlos: There are 100% of people on the Internet. Then there's this big social network.

Dana: Let's use Twitter.

Carlos: Okay, Twitter, if you look at the top influencers on Twitter 20% of them are driving 80% of the content.

Dana: So those 20% are the ones creating most of the content.

Carlos: Finding the influencer who's going to be effective is an intricate approach. What should you be looking for when examining their followers? Not the traditional reach which is simply the number of followers. What you need to be looking for is the core of that following.

I once headed a campaign with a major celebrity to promote a show. This celebrity had double-digit millions in followers. I did the same type of campaign with a couple of women who had 4 to 6 million followers. The 4-6 million had a 400% higher engagement than the celebrity with ten times the number of followers. The **core** of the 4-6 million followers was more passionate and engaged.

Dana: With a more engaged core.

Carlos: The 4-6 million followers of the women fit into the category that was most receptive to their core message. They were speaking the right message to the right audience.

Dana: When I'm aware of my core audience and speak in a voice that's specific to them, organically more engagement will happen.

Carlos: It's like this, if you're standing at a concert jumping up and screaming, how many people are listening to you? Probably not too many – because those other people are doing their own thing at the concert – maybe jumping up and screaming also. Now, if you're in a small room and you're jumping and screaming, how many people are going to listen to you?

Dana: Everyone in the room will be looking at me.

Carlos: Exactly. And for a brand it's about focusing on a targeted audience, building scalability through a network of influencers that have, as their core audience, the followers that you want to reach. Casting a wide net and hoping that you'll hook people is much less effective – and more costly – than researching the right audience for your brand and targeting them via the influencers they are engaging with regularly.

Carlos Sapene and Dana C. Arnett

6
TYPES OF CONTENT

Carlos: Let's start by understanding one thing, 'content is king'. For brands, content is a way to communicate with their audience. There's a lot of storytelling that can be done through content. Aside from just providing information, the right content can create a perception and through that perception, the brand has an opportunity to become an authority and build trust. Original content builds on a concept, whereas curated content repurposes a concept to create perspective. Either one, used correctly, can build an effective strategy to deliver the message.

When we're talking curating, we understand that there's a wealth of content that's available on the Internet. What we're saying is, you don't need to reinvent the wheel all the time. The first thing to do is understand what your message is. In what way would people align with that message and who out there is delivering that message through their content? It could even be that a single piece of content inspired you to want to associate your brand to it. Then part of the work is finding similarities with your brand or interpretations that are applicable to what other people have already created. Far from plagiarism, to repurpose (not copy) content using your brand voice associates you to the message or inspiration the piece of content delivers.

Dana: Let's say I'm a bottling company and I want to use content from the web to give visibility to my product and I want to use curated content.

Carlos: The first thing we want to determine, who's your audience?

Dana: People who like to drink soda.

Carlos: Okay, now what types of people drink soda?

Dana: Young people, eighteen to twenty-five.

Carlos: And what is your message?

Dana: Mine is the best cola for your summer!

Carlos: 'The best cola for your summer!' Now, find out how people are interpreting the best ways to spend their summer. What are their best moments from the summer? Then you can associate the information gathered with your brand. Your brand is set on providing the best moments of summer.

Maybe it's someone proposing to his or her girlfriend on the beach during the summer? Maybe it's someone's graduation party or birthday? You can gather all of these and begin to create a picture of your message.

When people share content on social media they understand that it is public, unless they've purposefully set it to private. By you having the ability to re-tweet it, re-post it and share it both you and the content creator benefit. They receive more views and you craft your curated perception, your brand story.

Dana: The brand is looking for a way to emotionally connect with the audience by using something that is already there. We're inserting ourselves into your great experience in a way or vice versa. The goal is to bring our soda into your summer.

Carlos: That's how a brand can use curated content on social media to help craft a message to their desired audience.

Dana: If I'm a brand that desires a unique message, all my own, that's original content by a content creator.

Carlos: A content creator, which is what most influencers are, has a far more aggressive growth curve to stardom than traditional 'celebrities'. It's the authenticity of the message and the organic nature of the creative process that appeals to people. The influencer is an 'expert' and believes in the content that they're creating. Therefore there's a much more honest disposition to the delivery.

Dana: This is precisely why it's not in a brand's best interest to hire just any group of influencers. You hire specific influencers whose voice and message resonates in the area of the targeted audience you want to reach.

Carlos: Then you work with these influencers to build content. The opportunity here is that because they know how to speak to that audience in a unique way that's genuine, they will craft content that will deliver the message effectively.

Native Content = Seeing But Not Knowing

Carlos: Native is a younger form of advertising. On the web people have become accustomed to traditional display advertising. If we go back and look at how overall marketing strategy has evolved, we might start with billboards.

Dana: I looked this up: Billboards were a successful form of advertising even before the 1900's. Then the Model-T came along and that created a new mobile audience that could be marketed to. They were placed at the sides of roads to capture the attention of passing motorists.

Carlos: There were humongous billboards like the Marlboro Man placed on Sunset Boulevard and in Time's Square. They were a big deal and hugely successful marketing during their time. That is the same basic concept that initially made display advertising effective on the web.

All advertising media goes through the same cycle and based on what time in history they appear, that cycle restarts. The latest cycle, which I like to call the traditional marketing cycle, evolved from the billboards on streets into TV advertisements. As people got used to the billboards, they became less effective and began to develop a sort of blindness to them. More so with the onset of television, which drew the eyeballs in a new way from the street to the screen and integrated the advertisements into the flow of content building on the association of the content to the placement of the ad.

The same is true with the appearance of the Internet. As fast as the Internet moves, it is still at a standard pace for how it's evolved. With more and more eyeballs moving to the smaller screen, we had to devise a way to integrate advertising into the line-of-sight. What better way than some 'traditional' billboards or banners, which is what they came to be called. Repeating the billboard cycle, we began to learn to ignore the banners on our screens. We went from the banner ads on web pages to developing 'banner blindness'*.

Banner Blindness *is a phenomenon in web usability where visitors to a website consciously or subconsciously ignore* **banner***-like information, which can also be called ad* **blindness** *or* **banner** *noise.*

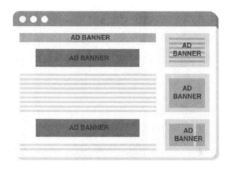

Carlos: Advertisements on websites are placed in specific positions; there's the top of the website, the right side of the website (called the right rail) and the bottom of an article. These are the traditional spots for advertisers. In the early days, editorial teams, were very hesitant to mix in any sort of advertisement with the content. It was all about editorial integrity.

Dana: To not throw an ad in the middle of an article.

Carlos: Yes. It's considered misleading or a bait-and-switch type of deception. The Federal Trade Commission or FTC is a government body that has been aggressive about the disclosure of advertising, particularly when built into content. They want to make sure people know the difference when they're reading something objective and when they're being sold something.

Dana: Recently we've been seeing an uptick in enforcement as well as now seeing "Paid Sponsor" or "Paid Content" at the end of articles or when influencers are talking about something they are being paid for. The FTC is becoming very strict so that consumers are aware when Native Advertising is being used.

Carlos: What Native Content has done is change the conversation. The true purpose of Native Advertising is that brands attach themselves to content that is relevant, and objective for their audience, their core. Instead of only having a banner around a piece of content, have someone build content that promotes their brand by associating it to knowledge of the subject matter or providing value on a specific topic. For example, in the case of a financial advertiser, the content they would pay to have written would be an article about "The Ten Best Ways To Save Your Money". That is a great example of Native Content.

Dana: Or, "How to Invest your Money", "How to Build a Solid Retirement".

Carlos: Exactly. The traditional banner display was a one-way type of advertising that was literally in your face. The banner had flash animation and pop-ups that exploded on your screen.

Dana: Like what AOL was doing.

Carlos: AOL. Yes and many others. It was very much in your face, forcing you, trying to force you to look at the app.

Dana: Look at me! Look at me!

Carlos: There's still some of that but it's lost its effectiveness. Then there's still the concept of incentivized viewing, the idea that 'I won't let you through to my site until you watch this video' or sign-up for something. It's called incentivized; I call it arm-twisting.

Dana: That bothers me!

Carlos: Do people really want to watch that video? No, you're forcing me and what do you think I'll remember about your brand?

Dana: That your brand annoyed me.

Carlos: And forced me to watch this stupid video. Most people press play, walk away and come back later; they're still not watching the video. Some of the players in Native Content have tried to force that as well, in order to gain viewership and build up numbers. We call them 'black hat' players as we referred to earlier. There's also the 'white hat players' that are the ones that are really working to build up content that provides value to the consumer.

The White Hats = The Good Guys

Dana: Well that's because they're the good guys. Hopefully the ones in the marketplace that use the tools and skills that are out there to bring their brand to an audience or vice versa. The brand is not looking at the audience simply as a means to an end. They're not saying 'buy my product' or 'look here now', but actually give me something that is worth my taking the time to read.

Carlos: Exactly. The user is giving you their time and attention, that's their value. Why wouldn't you give them something back or give them something of value to remember you by? Then when I'm setting up my savings account I'm actually thinking of this bank that was the one that told me how to do all of this in an article they curated or created. I'm probably going to go to that bank, because they're the ones that helped me to understand what I needed to do.

Dana: They took the time to give you some valuable tools.

Carlos: They took the time to help me through it and I'm going to have a positive perception of that bank. In my experience, having been associated with a white hat player in this field, they are the ones that are really trying to build content that provides a value. You can see that long-term strategy being more sustainable than trying to force people to relate to something.

Dana: By aggressively manipulating them.

Carlos: Websites that are running the black-hat ads are losing the value of the position of those ads. What brands are realizing is 'if I go that route with those sites that are implementing this type of advertising, even though they are calling it native, it's not' ...

Dana: It may harm my brand.

Carlos: The publishers that have the sites that are allowing these types of ads are harming the brands and their long-term value. If

I'm charging you fourteen dollars per thousand video views and you're getting zero return on it, you're not going to want to pay fourteen dollars for those thousand people that don't want to watch your ad.

Whereas, if you're reaching your core audience and getting a high rate of return because you're engaging people, you'll gladly pay fourteen dollars. People that are reading your content are reading it because they care to learn about that subject and they're connecting your brand to this substantial information. Your rate of return is fifty percent higher than traditional cases of display advertising.

Correcting the Alignment

Dana: Let's run through a hypothetical example. The automaker Hummer hires a digital marketing team to gather influencers and promote a new car campaign. The team does the research but mistakenly ends up hiring an influencer that is a non-driving, green-touting, avid walker who doesn't believe in the automobile as a mode of transportation. They hire this influencer to talk about the new (gas-guzzling) Hummer, what will the influencers followers do?

Carlos: First of all, I'm guessing you're not a gas-guzzling car lover? LOL. If the influencer were smart they would never take that gig. Because as an influencer the worst thing you can do is violate the trust of your following by going counter to your beliefs. The moment followers see you as disingenuous, the moment they feel cheated by you, they're gone. That's the moment your followers will choose to abandon you.

Dana: If followers get even a whiff of you using them to make money…

Carlos: …some will un-follow you and in most cases your Active Followers will be quite vocal about it!

Dana: Influencers should research every brand that approaches them. You could blow your career (and business) as an influencer by not aligning with appropriate brands.

Carlos: It goes for both sides of the transaction. Brands have to work with the right influencers to reach the appropriate core audiences, just as much as influencers need to work with the right brands that appeal to them and their audience. I've seen influencers that have taken to telling people that they're promoting something for the money. They decided to prevent people seeing them as disingenuous. And now it's required by the FTC. That's why it's even more important that it aligns with who you are.

Dana: That's why we're careful when we work with brands and influencers. We're transparent in order to make sure that everybody is in sync and above board. We often put together appropriate groups of influencers and we leverage that to help the brand with a broader reach.

Carlos: That works because we're maximizing the targeted reach. What we want to do here is find pools of interested people. It's like crab fishing; you're looking for where you can get the most pounds of crab, not just randomly casting out into the ocean hoping a crab will be there somewhere. And that right there… was a native ad for our agency ;)

Annoying Marketing Methods

Carlos: People have learned about disruptive ads, well maybe they're not disruptive but they're annoying, that's what they are. I would call Native disruptive in a different way. Disruptive marketing is not about disrupting your day; it's about disrupting the way that information is delivered and the perception it leaves behind after it's consumed.

Dana: Disruptive is about presenting new ways to get us to view or read something and that's NOT by annoying us.

Carlos: It's about your thinking, your perceptions. Creating perception is a huge part of marketing. Brands know how annoying these things are.

Dana: Many women enjoy reading about the latest diet. If it says 'diet', we click. Recently, I started reading, "The Ten New Ways To Exercise Off That Ankle Fat."

Carlos: Wait... what?

Dana: They were citing doctors about the number of calories I needed to burn and explaining why ankle fat is so stubborn. I'm thinking, "Wow...who knew?" The doctor talked about an herbal remedy recommended to patients to specifically target the ankle. That's when I started getting suspicious. Suddenly I'm scrolling to reveal an ad at the bottom of the article for that exact herbal remedy! Now I'm annoyed with myself that I got lured in and I realize, I've just done EXACTLY what they wanted me to do! Then I feel manipulated and I really don't like them.

Carlos: I call those, the half and halfs, they're half native and half display advertising. When brands unsuccessfully manipulate their audience it's only natural for people to associate that brand with deceitfulness.

Dana: You bet, one hundred percent.

Carlos: Native is about providing value and then associating your brand with the value. We would have provided the information from the doctors, except before you even started reading the article; there would be a clear disclosure that it's a sponsored piece of content. That way you know that you're getting value, and an expert brings it to you.

There is an 80/20 test with the FTC. They sit a group of users in front of a piece of advertising. Native or otherwise. More than eighty percent of the users have to be able to identify the ad as an advertisement when they view it. If they are not able to, then you are potentially in for a lawsuit or at the very least a hefty fine. The FTC is focused on these types of advertisements now, going not only after the brands that violate the 80/20 but also after the agencies that sell them these concepts. It's about protecting the consumer and the integrity of information.

Dana: They are trying to stop people from being duped.

Carlos: The 'fat ankle' article that you read was great, but then..

Dana: It flipped.

Carlos: It flipped.

Dana: Suddenly I get a hit and I go, 'something just changed'. I then feel gullible. I feel completely taken.

Carlos: It would have been better to have the article written and then have an additional piece of information at the bottom with a different color background that endorses the brand. Not as part of the article. It's disingenuous. It kills brand trust. Those strategies are also strategies that are used more by black or grey hat marketers. It may 'work' in the short term but it hurts both the brand and advertising overall in the long term.

Carlos Sapene and Dana C. Arnett

7
KNOWING YOUR BRAND AUDIENCE

Dana: The same ideas around influencers finding their audiences are also around brands finding theirs. It's the same discovery strategy. There are basic questions to ask such as, "Who am I selling this product to?" and "What type of people are interested in using my product?"

Carlos: "How will they receive it?" A company can pay a ton of money making pretty ads with great content but if they're pushing the brand and not targeting to the correct audience, they might as well keep the money in the bank.

Organic or Pre-Meditated

Carlos: The funny thing is, some brands already organically have influencers that they haven't capitalized on yet. There's influencers out there already talking about a brand and the brand doesn't necessarily know that it's happening. It's an incredible gift if that's occurring so it's important to go look at those people, listen to and engage them. Finding if there's already an audience out there and discover those influencers. Who are they reaching? How many are listening? How many people are talking about this?

The traditional approach is to go straight to the marketing plan asking questions like: How are we going to push this? Where are we going to push this? Where are the sites that massive groups of people are reading?

Dana: One of the things I love most about the digital business is that people can already be talking about you and it didn't cost you a dime. To your point, it's worth the research to see if people are already invested in your brand and who they are. We do so much research and reporting before creating a strategy. We can tell what's effective and what's not and who's already giving a voice to your brand. How fortunate that people started talking and you were already developing an audience before you even knew it!

Before digital you put an ad in a magazine and you didn't know if anybody came to your store because of that ad. You were just hoping that it did well.

Carlos: In the digital space advertising is now very different. Why? Because information and data are available and everything can be researched to create an effective campaign if you know how to interpret and use the data correctly. In the white hat area, data is extremely useful. There's re-target marketing, where you look at a pair of shoes on Zappos, later on you're reading a news story on CNN and there's an ad with the same shoes on the page.

Dana: The Zappos site has captured the data on what shoes we've looked at and they're putting them where we're now looking. It's happening right now with Appleletics – our Internet retail client. We drive the consumer to their website, they click on a pair of yoga pants and those pants follows them to other websites they view.

Carlos: Re-targeting has saved display advertising, for now. It's been an evolution of display advertising where we've understood that people who have demonstrated interest in something are far more willing to interact with it than those who haven't. People stopped looking at those ad boxes on the page, but when the corner of your eye catches the shoe or pant you stared at 30 minutes ago, you're going to look over there. That's how banners became a more personal type of advertising. The same is true for influencers. If you've expressed interest in a topic, you're far more likely to listen to them again.

Dana: Facebook and Google helped pave the way because they started collecting big data on interests and intention.

Carlos: They collect everything you do and what you like and then they re-sell the data. Facebook re-sells the use of the data through their system but they don't re-sell it with any PII*.

*PII *is Personal Identifiable Information*

Big data opens the door to specific and interest-based advertisements. You're able to sell it as a package. With big data you can say, "We have women, women who like shoes and women who liked these shoes in the past three days." But it's never anything that personally identifies you.

Dana: It won't say it's your name or where you live. Thankfully.

Carlos: Exactly. The FTC is very particular about no collection or distribution of PII. You can get into trouble for giving out PII. It's dangerous to have that type of information. There are many ways to restrict people from gathering that information from you.

At the end of the day, there are certain lines we shouldn't cross when using data and when used correctly, it is a highly effective way to bring your product to people. It is another level of influencing your audience.

Dana: It's still all about what you're doing for me and using data like this is basically making it easier for me to make a purchase if it's something I want. We always go back to the tenet of influence that says 'your followers choose you. You do not choose your followers'. And if you put it under my nose I may just follow the cookie!

Carlos: Somehow I don't remember that last portion about the cookie. Nevertheless, brands deliver value then the influencer delivers value and with that, their audience goes and buys your product. When it's right, it's the perfect marriage.

Dana: Using influencers to deliver a message is more effective than traditional marketing tactics?

Carlos: There's a reason why traditional marketing uses reach, they want to target a lot of people. Their desire is to get the most people possible to buy a product so they spend a lot of money doing exactly that. However, because there is no way to identify that you're reaching the right people with your money...

Dana: ...they cast a wide net.

Carlos: It's a huge net! Huge. Like I said about the crab, I will restate it and say 'you need to fish where the fish are, but you also need to fish where the fish are that you want to catch!' There's no point in catching fish that you won't eat.

The moment you have a subset of influencers with the audience you're after and that are part of their core, you start building true reach. You're reaching the right people with the right message. You could be reaching a hundred thousand people but only have twenty people connecting with your brand. At that point you're losing money and time. But talking to three hundred targeted people where two hundred and eighty of them are willing to connect or discover your brand – now THAT'S great marketing.

Dana: Much better use of time and money. This is why brands need professionals who know how to target.

8
TARGET MARKETING
AND
SOCIAL MEDIA CHANNELS

Dana: Let's look at data targeting and why boosting a post through advertising or influencers is not as effective if you're not targeting the right audience.

Carlos: Data has the ability to capture an audience and grow it tremendously. Over time people have released their hold on privacy which has allowed marketers to enhance their ability to target people with the right messaging in the right places.

One of the things to keep in mind is this: Facebook, as an example, gives you the ability to send targeted messaging to specific groups of people within a social network and through it's audience network which extends beyond their walled world to apps and websites that are approved to carry Facebook ads. You can look at your desired audience and sub-segment them. For instance, "I'm going to develop this type of messaging for mothers on Facebook and I'm going to develop a different type of messaging for Millennials on Facebook. I'm going to develop this type of messaging for people that have said that they like my brand in the past on Facebook". With those three different types of messages under one campaign you're able to be specific with your target.

Target Marketing Example

Dana: Let's say I have a t-shirt business that's geared towards college students that are the perfect audience for my shirts. How would we advertise on social media?

Carlos: What would be your focus? It's your brand and if you were targeting only college students, what would your personal message be?

Dana: Well...I could suggest, "This shirt will help you hook up!" I know more than just college students are interested in hooking up. Maybe it's an age range I'm looking at and not only college students?

Carlos: What you're looking for and why I think this is a great exercise is that you're looking at what *your* t-shirt/brand should do. Before you go and try to market in the social media world, you need to know what your brand is about and what you want to put out there. How do you want to represent your brand? What do you want to say about your shirts? The biggest mistake is to put the concept of your brand in the hands of your marketer and abdicate responsibility.

Dana: Because it could go anywhere. Or nowhere.

Carlos: They can take you anywhere since you don't have any idea where you want to go – your marketing dollars can be diluted without a proper target. Before you go out there and start planning your social strategy, identify what your brand is about. What is your brand going to represent? Who are the audiences for your brand?

Then you can start finding influencers that your brand would appeal to.

Let's run through an exercise together. What I want you to do is go get a piece of paper and write down what your brand is about. It should be no more than two sentences.

It's said that if anything takes longer than 5 minutes to explain it's not worth explaining, so keep it simple:

1. Write down your brand.
2. Write down what your brand represents to you.
3. Put down audiences that you think would want to wear your brand

So let's say it's 18-34 and 18-22 are college students. Maybe from those college students you want to send a different message to females than to males. Because even if 'hooking up' is your message, it's a different message in how you reach that audience effectively. You also want to target people who THINK like they're still college students. They are maybe past the age of 22 and are between 22 and 34.

Dana: Obviously it's not just college age students who are flirting and going to bars.

Carlos: You need to determine the key things attached to that group like flirting, youthful, fun, dating, going to bars etc. You want to define as deeply as possible the audience for your shirts. This is the step that will give you the basis of your marketing strategy.

Dana: Define the audience for your product first. Examine the social channels and the different types of strategies and audiences that align with each of those channels, and see if your audience is there. That's how you find out where to start. Then learn how to talk to them in the language of that channel.

Carlos: Developing your strategy for social media is in knowing what type of content needs to go into each social network. A *common marketing mistake* is to view all social networks as a single channel. Social networks create engagement and each person engages through each medium for a different reason. If you look at how you behave on a social network you'll understand why we're saying that you need to define a social strategy for each Social Media platform. For example, on Facebook, we're used to relating with family and friends and catching up with what they're doing. It enforces a voyeuristic nature by allowing us to keep up with people in a very personal way.

FACEBOOK

The social media messaging on Facebook should be structured in a very personal way, like you're talking to your friends. It's a place where you can tug at people's heartstrings or ask them to celebrate with you. It's a place where you talk to your friends and family in a voice that they can identify as you. It's not a place where you're providing 'important' information and saying, "Click here for more." It's a place where people are drawn in in a personal way by sharing experiences.

Dana: What I do love about Facebook is that I can keep up with people that I haven't seen in years. We don't even have to engage with each other outside of Facebook. It gives us the ability to get to know people emotionally and connect with them whether we've seen them recently or not.

Carlos: It's a personal platform. Then you have to look at your brand and ask what elements of the brand make it personal? What makes it something of interest to the person that's looking at it or reading about it?

TWITTER

Carlos: Twitter is a hundred and forty characters and imagery. It's developed into a visual social network platform with the ability to incorporate images and social video. Twitter is about rapid communication. It's about newsy type content and not about engaging people in a long conversation.

Dana: Sound bites.

Carlos: Sound bites exactly - a great way to look at it. Now you have to ask how you are going to reach people that are on the go? How are you going to engage them with your brand? This sums up the difference between Facebook and Twitter.

Dana: On Facebook you have the time, on Twitter you don't have the time. So you have to craft your messaging in a way that it's delivering the most bang for your buck in a hundred and forty characters and/or one image and/or one video.

Carlos: Crafting a message for a brand depends on the brand and it depends on the personality. When you're developing strategies you don't implement them without talking to someone first. It could be a friend, a relative - someone who thinks differently than you do.

Sometimes we get so close to our brand that we can lose objectivity – it's natural. That's why talking to others is essential for objectivity. There's an assumption that people are going to know certain things about your brand. There may be an assumption that people already believe certain things about your brand, but it's only an assumption and you always need an impartial perspective.

Dana: Objective feedback is crucial.

Carlos: Run it by a few people that think differently because objectivity will inform your campaign. You should craft your message from the perspective of your audience, not *your* perspective as the seller.

SNAPCHAT

Carlos: Let's talk about the use of quick visual content, as in Snapchat. One of the biggest mistakes some marketers make is to assume that because a social network is different from what they are used to, it's not going to be useful or worse, that it's going to fail. It's a challenge to learn a new platform, to see outside the box but that's what makes digital media exciting. How many people bet on Facebook and Twitter? I have no idea, but the point is that innovation is a good thing and in that way you can open up a new world to your brand. In the beginning, many disregarded Snapchat. What some people might not know is that most social networks, at least the successful ones, evolve from something that may not seem appealing at first. Snapchat began as a short-snap for video and evolved to become a social video platform, which revolutionized video consumption and actually coined the term 'Social Video'.

Dana: People wondered how Snapchat could get anyone interested in messaging when in 10 seconds that piece of content would be deleted after it was been played.

Carlos: It's introduced a new discipline - in that amount of time you have to be able to communicate your message.

Dana: Discovering how to communicate in new ways makes for great creativity!

Carlos: It's necessary to evolve our thinking regarding the function of advertising in digital. It's not about getting a single message out there once. It's about getting multiple messages out there. Brands can utilize some of the advantages that have been developed on these platforms and be creative in their advertising.

Dana: It's so important to be creative and open. We live in a time that requires very flexible thinking.

Carlos: Understanding the technology, its limitations and its capabilities are of the utmost importance – then you can find your entry point. The most effective marketing is now digital marketing. You have to adapt because it's just not the same as it used to be. Take YouTube for example. With YouTube, people see it as a video hub. They forget that YouTube is the second largest search engine in the world – over 3 billion searches a month.

Dana: After Google.

Carlos: After Google and beating Bing. You create content for YouTube and you have to craft it for an audience that is going to engage with short quality content. With advertisers on YouTube, you have an even shorter amount of time to engage the user.

YOUTUBE

Carlos: There are a couple of options for advertising on YouTube; you can skip the ad after three seconds (a pre-roll ad to market) or the smarter way is to actually work with influencers. The impressive difference is, you're using an already established and trusted voice to deliver your message.

One major challenge moving out of traditional marketing is that we're so used to controlling the voice, controlling the output, controlling the messaging and controlling the delivery of the message. In this new digital world, you don't have those constraints and if you want to be effective, you shouldn't have those constraints. With influencers, there's a reason why they have become who they are and why hoards of people are following them.

Dana: It's changed marketing. It's organic and it's appealing.

Carlos: Gen-X is still used to looking at stars on the red carpet, but you talk to the Millennial generation and they know more about Pudie Pie than Nicole Ritchie. It's necessary for brands to take into consideration that Millennials look at "celebrity" differently. Celebrity endorsements that we looked at and used before are not as valuable because the field has broadened to include Internet kids that are just doing their thing, showcasing it on YouTube and people becoming interested in them.

I think you see more and more people not only looking to celebrities as role models. The younger generations are looking at influencers on YouTube and other social networks in that regard.

Dana: Because they feel real to them.

Carlos: Because they think they can be them. The younger generations identify more with real people. The glamour of celebrity doesn't seem to be as appealing. Many young people see it as glamour and excess and they are looking to people they can identify with who speak their language.

Dana: And of course, being a real person is certainly more attainable for the masses.

Carlos: Social media and marketing are affected by the economy. Of course people will relate more with a person who shares their struggles than a celebrity shopping on Rodeo Drive. We've moved into a different stage of engaging with people. As a brand, to engage people on YouTube the best way is to partner with content creators, influencers. You work with them to co-create content to distribute through YouTube. That's going to be far more effective for your brand than creating a pre-rolled ad and running it before a video.

Dana: Let's go back to the t-shirt example. If I want to target 18-24 college students and I've flushed out all my reasons why they fit my brand, then it would be smart for me to find an influencer in my key demographic on YouTube that would be interested in wearing a sexy t-shirt that says whatever. This would be a better use of time and money than trying to 'advertise' the shirt somewhere.

Carlos: Exactly.

Dana: Because that influencer's audience is the audience you want to target. Reaching out to influencer's is a smart marketing move. It's better for the brand and beneficial to the person on YouTube.

Carlos: In that example though, you're still thinking as a regular marketer, because you're thinking product placement.

Dana: Good point.

Carlos: You're thinking, I'm just going to have them wear my shirt and that's going to make everyone want to buy it. Now you might get lucky, but rather than just put the shirt on someone, having an influencer discuss your shirt as a point of topic will bring more sales. In some cases, it's more beneficial to have the YouTuber make fun of your shirt than wear it.

Dana: It goes back to valuing honesty and authenticity. Any press is good press?

Carlos: By you letting them be who they are, their followers will make their own decisions about buying that particular shirt. We're in a time now that there isn't good PR and bad PR, there's just PR. All you need is somebody that's going to be heard. These people are heard. Just because they make fun of a t-shirt, it doesn't mean that people won't buy the shirt. It sometimes means that people will want the shirt even more. Ironic sales are better than no sales.

INSTAGRAM

Carlos: Instagram is an evolving method of storytelling. Instagram is visual. The ad opportunities on Instagram are interesting because they allow you to create a story through imagery. The way that I look at Instagram, do you remember when we were kids and we had those things that looked like binoculars?

Dana: Yes, the ViewMaster had the cards with the little photos on them.

Carlos: And you could click it and you would view them one by one. That's what an Instagram ad is. If you're able to look at your story in that circle, you can create an Instagram ad that's effective. It's visual. It's story-telling. It's a slideshow. You're able to get your point across in a creative way. It's multiple images, but you're swiping through them.

Dana: Let's review what we've covered for the current social media platforms:

Carlos: Ok, here's an easy breakdown:

> **Facebook** is personal.
>
> **Twitter** is short and creative.
>
> **YouTube** is about engaging in a creative way through the trusted voices present on YouTube.
>
> **Instagram** is about story-telling through imagery.
>
> **SnapChat** is about short bursts of video that are front-loaded with information.
>
> **Periscope** is talking directly and in the present moment to an audience.

Dana: That should make it very clear that you can't have one strategy for every social platform!

Periscope - A Big Impact?

Carlos: Whether or not it's Periscope, or something like it is still being debated. Meerkat launched first. Twitter bought Periscope - reports say for over $75 million - and to stifle the competition they blocked Meerkat from having access to their fire hose – basically to all of Twitter.

Dana: It just shows the war for control of these new innovative social networks is always on.

Carlos: Periscope has capitalized on the worldwide voyeuristic nature of people. It scratches the itch of wanting to understand and communicate with other cultures since it's a global experience.

Periscope is opening the United States' ability to understand countries better, like Iran. If you look at Iran from the media perspective, the first feeling that comes to mind is, 'enemy'.

Dana: That's maybe how the media has influenced our perception.

Carlos: What Periscope has allowed is for people in this country to see people in another country as individuals. It's also provided a new way to access live news and relevant content in a timely manner.

Dana: Not just dramatic newsy things but people doing everyday stuff.

Carlos: Scopers show that all people have regular lives like we do - families, and playtime, dinner with friends, school etc.

Dana: We get to see a wide variety of people like street vendors and business owners in another country.

Carlos: What Periscope is doing is far more than creating a social network; it's really building a connection. A human connection I haven't seen in this capacity on a social network.

Dana: The exposure is different because it's live and now Facebook is doing it too. You can see people just being themselves. The black hats have not yet corrupted Periscope.

Carlos: No, not yet but it won't be long before brands will insert themselves in there. It'll probably be through advertising.

Dana: For now, live streaming on Periscope feels very fresh and genuine.

Carlos: Think about it this way, Facebook allows you to be voyeuristic with your friends while not having to be in contact. How many people do you keep up with on Facebook that you don't talk to? You may think you know everything about them because you see everything that they do on Facebook. Why would you need to call them? Last night I had dinner with a friend I haven't seen for a year, yet everything that she brought up I already knew from Facebook.

Dana: It happens to me all the time. Just last year at my High School reunion, I knew exactly how many kids my former classmates had, and their ages. You can watch their lives, but you don't need to engage in it.

Carlos: You perceive that you know everything about them. You perceive that these are still your friends, but you don't have a complete picture of someone only through pictures and posts. With Periscope, you're getting a live person, a live interaction and a live connection.

Now, we're extending these connections worldwide. It gives

broader access to the world and communication. This has led to the evolution we see in the consumption of news and media. That's why younger generations are watching Fox News, CNN, and MSNBC less and less...because they have the tools to see beyond what's being fed to them.

It's too early to comment on whether Periscope is going to be a game changer. Periscope may very well be the MySpace of live video broadcasting. What Periscope is doing though is it's opening us up to a cultural exchange and a worldwide view. Periscope is on its way to being the most honest and transparent marketing media. You have no choice but to be yourself. You have to be on there being yourself and you're going to be your own brand.

Dana: You're a human, not a business. You're a person or you're a group of friends or you're part of a group of people. You're just living your life and exposing people to that.

Carlos: For those that understand that and are able to capitalize on that and turn it into a strategy, the effect is immense. How do I represent both myself and my passion for my brand through this new medium? These are the ones that are going to be successful on this live stream.

Dana: They'll turn into influencers.

Carlos: Streaming, yes, live video streaming on Periscope or whatever that social network ends up being.

Dana: It's technically brilliant and conceptually simple.

Carlos: Yeah, the execution is brilliant. It's still a challenge to not stifle innovation and turn it into a business. At the end of the day, Periscope has already developed a new construct. It's the reality TV of social media entertainment. Periscope has popularized live broadcast and they've focused on keeping it as just that, but live broadcast will just become part of the experience, as will VR (Virtual Reality). It will be built in as another function. Much like Facebook is doing by adding it to their stream of content. Although knowing Facebook, they'll later try and break that out into it's own app. But that's the subject for another book.

Dana: I think that's the normal evolution of most everything. What about using Periscope as a strategy?

Carlos: If you can capitalize on Periscope or Facebook live, with a strategy of transparency and honesty while showing your brand and your passion, you will have a great chance at succeeding as an influencer in a social network that's going to lead a type of interaction that will become an integral part of how we interact worldwide. Know that influencers tend to survive, thrive and migrate together through social media, so the death of one network is nothing but the birth of another.

Dana: When you lay eyes on the vast landscape across all media platforms, it's easy to see why one would need to hire a marketing company!

Carlos: Like us (ah we just slipped in some native).

Dana: Yes, we see all sides of how brands can be helped and harmed. How influencers can help or harm them. I'll restate what

I learned years ago to 'hire what you don't know' meaning, you don't have to try and figure everything out yourself. Do what you do best and hire what you don't know. It ends up saving time and money.

Carlos: And whether it's us or not, it's important to find professionals who know how to execute these strategies. What we've learned most over time is that nothing about marketing is a one-size-fits-all strategy and hiring the right influencers, making the right deals for both brand and influencer, is paramount to ensure a mutually beneficial campaign. Then the possibilities are unlimited.

9
THE INFLUENCER ELEVATOR PITCH

Dana: I think we should wrap up our book with a traditional elevator pitch which is a 'succinct and persuasive sales pitch'. Since we don't need to 'sell' anyone on anything, how about just giving me something succinct to describe influencer marketing.

Let's say we're having coffee in an elevator and I have no idea about marketing or digital except maybe my digital watch. I only know that I read and buy stuff on my computer. Without spilling your coffee, what's your elevator pitch that explains influencer marketing to me?

Carlos: Influencer marketing is like sitting in a room with a bunch of your friends having cocktails. You start telling a story and you have a captive audience interested in listening because they enjoy you and they like what you have to say. They may align themselves with your beliefs and the way you see life. You're all friends.

Dana: It's too esoteric – I don't get it.

Carlos: Your friends like you – you influence them. It's aligning yourself with the person in the room that's going to tell a story that you're interested in hearing because of who's telling it. It's genuine storytelling through people that are speaking to an audience that cares to hear what they have to say.

Dana: OK, stop and please try again. You know I like examples –

that explanation was a little too vague. I'm leaving the elevator soon.

Carlos: Ok, here you go: You and I are at a party and we're in the living room with a group of friends. We're telling a story about the fact that we're writing a book. I'm talking and telling the story right now, and I'm telling it from my perspective. The group is sitting there nodding and wanting to check out the book. Because they like and trust me, they are interested in the things that I'm saying. I'm the one telling the story therefore I'm the influencer.

Dana: So a couple of things are happening at the party: YOU (the Influencer) are telling the story to the GROUP (the Followers) and because they like you and are listening to what you have to say and are interested, they are going to go buy our book (the Product). Then they will hopefully talk about it to others (word-of-mouth Advertising) and our 'followers' will grow.

That pitch was much better – I got a good party visual.

Carlos: It's really not that complicated. Now let's finish this darn book so our friends can go buy it.

ABOUT THE AUTHORS

CARLOS SAPENE

CHIEF DIGITAL OFFICER, WICKED BIONIC

Carlos has built a career helping some of the most recognizable brands in the entertainment, fashion and music industries - like E!, Style Network and Bravo - learn, understand and grow their audiences using the Internet. Carlos started in technology, learning the ins-and-out of the famous back-ends of systems and in some cases building them from scratch. Throughout the years he grew into marketing and product development, working on some of the biggest social media campaigns and advertising products. From soup to nuts, he has either built it, designed it, marketed it or used it.

His focus now is applying his knowledge to help clients build successful Internet businesses by combining SEO, Internet and Influencer marketing, advertising and big data. Having grown websites from 400,000 unique users to over 19 million, his strategies have proven to be effective in significantly reducing the cost of customer acquisition.

Carlos lives in Los Angeles with his husband Edward Morgan and three awesome celebrity dogs: Bogie named after Humphrey Bogart, Elizabeth after Elizabeth Taylor and Ava after Ava Gardner...a group of followers.

DANA C. ARNETT

CHIEF OPERATING OFFICER, WICKED BIONIC

A long career in television and entertainment culminated in working as a VP in charge of Post Production at a Top 5 reality television company for over a decade. By providing oversight and guidance to hundreds of post production teams, over 400 series and pilots on multiple platforms were delivered to broadcast television and cable networks.

Dana is the structure and backbone of Wicked Bionic, managing client relationships, overseeing projects from inception to completion and beyond. The objective of the agency is long term client relations which Dana believes is achieved by quality performance and exceeding the goals on each project – and delivering on time and on budget.

Dana lives in Marina del Rey with her long-time partner Suzanne Hebert, a private practice Psychotherapist, and Yorkies Joey and Toby - two of the best little guys ever.

WICKED BIONIC

Wicked Bionic is an award-winning full service digital agency based in Los Angeles.

www.wickedbionic.com

38669845R00058

Made in the USA
San Bernardino, CA
10 September 2016